MONEY SAVING IDEAS

Guy Maasdorp.

Copyright Guy Maasdorp, 2012.
All Rights Reserved.
ISBN:978-1-300-13065-9

Information:

All products mentioned in this book are available from your local hardware and grocery store.

Meat Mincers are available from your local cater equipment company and spice packs, skins, etc. are available from your local spice merchant.

Scooters may be purchased from various manufacturers.

Backpacks, boots and other hiking equipment may be purchased from your local "Outdoor supplies store."

INTRODUCTION:

Most people spend a lot of time trying to work out how to make "extra income" instead of saving money on daily living which will earn you "extra income".

If you can earn 'extra income" and save money, then you have achieved the ultimate.

This book will show you how to earn "extra income" by implementing cost saving ideas.

CONTENTS:

Chapter 1. Make your own home care products……………………………….Pg 6

Chapter 2. Vegetables & Fruit……..Pg 8

Chapter 3. Meat………………….....Pg 10

Chapter 4. Water………………….. Pg 12

Chapter 5. Electricity……………....Pg 14

Chapter 6. Coldrinks…………….   Pg 16

Chapter 7. Barbeque…………….   Pg 18

Chapter 8. Haircuts………………   Pg 20

Chapter 9. Transport……………   Pg 21

Chapter 10. Vacations……………   Pg 22

Chapter 11. Home Schooling……   .Pg 24

Chapter 12. Work From Home…… Pg 26

Chapter 13. DIY…………………….Pg 27

Chapter 14. Internet Banking……   .Pg 28

Chapter 15. Motor Vehicle Repairs Pg 29

Chapter 16. Cutting Luxuries………Pg 31

Chapter 17. Home Generators… .   Pg 33

Chapter 18. Total Savings   …   Pg 35

CHAPTER 1 MAKE YOUR OWN HOME CARE PRODUCTS

1. Mould and Stain Remover

(60% Spirit of Salts, 20% Clean Green, 20% Water)

Requirements:

Plastic Spray Bottle, Funnel, Spirit of Salts, Clean Green.

Directions:

Add the Water first then the Clean Green then the Acid.

2. Toilet Cleaner

(40% Spirit of Salts, 20% Toilet Duck, 40% Water)

Requirements:

Plastic Spray Bottle, Toilet Duck, Spirit of Salts, Funnel.

Directions:

Add the Water first then the Toilet Duck then the Acid.

3. Drain Cleaner

(70% Pool Acid, 30% Water)

Requirements:

Plastic Squeeze Bottle, Gloves, Goggles, Pool Acid, Funnel.

Directions:

Wear Gloves and Goggles, Add the Water first then the Acid.

Total Requirements:

1. Funnel
2. Plastic Spray & Squeeze Bottles
3. Spirit of Salts
4. Pool Acid
5. Toilet Duck
6. Clean Green
7. Gloves
8. Goggles

This should save you approximately R200.00 per month = R2400.00 per annum = R168000.00 per lifetime of 70years.

CHAPTER 2 VEGETABLES AND FRUIT

Having a pretty garden with flowers is fine but having a pretty garden with vegetables and fruit trees is even better. There is nothing better than eating one's own home grown veggies and fruit. A small vegetable garden can keep a family of four with vegetables all year round. Home grown veggies and fruit are generally more nutritious and are healthier to eat than their bought counterparts. Flat or apartment dwellers also can grow their own by using trays with potting soil- these can be put on the balcony where they can enjoy some sunshine. The price of vegetables and fruit will never come down- they will only become more and more ridiculously expensive. Vegetables and fruit are vitally important for a balanced diet and are packed with vitamins. Some nutritionists maintain that raw veggies are the best and encourage kids to "graze" on them.

Fruit trees may be bought from your local nursery and vegetable seeds from your local hardware or grocery store. A lack of vegetables and fruit in one's diet can lead to all sorts of health problems including cancer. It's important to grow your vegetables which are in season- the back of the packet will tell you exactly when to plant. The type of soil prevalent in your area is also vitally important as certain vegetables and fruit only grow in certain soil conditions. Eating more vegetables and fruit will not only boost your health but will also help you to lose weight or maintain your current weight. It's also a great idea to make some meals without meat just using vegetables, fruit and pasta.

Start growing your own vegetables and fruit and keep your money in your wallet the next time you do grocery shopping.

This should save you approximately R200.00 per month = R2400 per annum = R168000 per 70 years lifetime.

CHAPTER 3 MEAT

Rule number 1 as far as meat is concerned is that you have to buy in bulk to achieve savings. Buying in small quantities from your local supermarket at ridiculous price per kg is just not acceptable.

The cheapest and perhaps the nicest meat to buy in bulk is game i.e. impala, kudu, springbok (buck). This may be purchased from your local butchery. Ask your butcher to cut your meat into steak, chops and stewing meat. Some people like to call it "wild meat" as it has a bit of a "wild" flavor. The "wild" flavor can be masked using garlic and butter when cooking and it tastes absolutely delicious. This meat is also very healthy to eat as it is thin and has no fat.

To obtain some variety and extend your meat supply and savings you will have to make your own mince and sausage. For this you will have to purchase a "meat mincer" from your local supplier. These may be purchased in mechanical or electrical forms. Further you will need "spice packs", "sausage skins" ,"punnet trays" and "plastic wrap" from your local supplier. To make your mince and sausage you need to purchase beef mince from a wholesaler as this will be the cheapest and make great sausage. To further extend your savings when making sausage you may add either "biscuit meal" or oats. My personal favorite is oats.

The "mincer" is a "one off" purchase which will more than pay for itself with the savings you gain.

This should save at least R200.00 per month = R2400.00 per annum = R168000.00 per 70 year lifetime.

CHAPTER 4 WATER

Rainwater is money from heaven- it is absolutely imperative for everyone to have a rainwater tank. Rainwater may be used throughout your home; all you need is a crossover switch to change to the municipal supply when necessary.

It will probably become a municipal law that all new and existing homes must have at least one rainwater tank. Even apartment blocks should have tanks to supply the residents.

Ensure taps are turned off and are not leaking-fix taps which are leaking. Shower rather than bath as this uses less water. Try and recycle water where possible.

Drinking water should only be rainwater as some municipal water is unfit for human consumption.

Watering the garden and washing one's car must be kept to a minimum.

Save water whenever and wherever possible.

Using a rainwater tank should save you R200.00 per month = R2400.00 per annum = R168000.00 per 70 year lifetime.

CHAPTER 5 ELECTRICITY

Any appliance either using heat or supplying heat draws the most current and uses the most electricity. Try and reduce or eliminate the usage of these appliances in the home.

The biggest electricity guzzler in your home is the geyser. To save electricity switch off the geyser during the day and switch on again in the evening before bath time. Solar geysers are also a big saver and are relatively inexpensive.

Switch off all non essential appliances at night e.g. a swimming pool pump or install a timer switch to automatically switch off.

Try to replace all the conventional bulbs in your external light fittings with energy efficient globes. These miniature- sized fluorescent tubes are extremely energy efficient, using up to 80% less electricity than a traditional incandescent light bulb while providing the same amount of light. A 14W energy efficient globe, for instance, has the same light output as a 60W incandescent bulb. They also last up to six times longer than an incandescent bulb- energy efficient globes will provide around 6000 hours of light compared with the 1000 hour operating lifespan of an incandescent bulb.

Another way to save energy is by fitting motion sensor lamps as security lighting instead of leaving a light burning all night long.

Employing these ideas could save you as much as **R200.00 per month = R2400.00 per annum = R168000.00** per 70 year lifetime.

CHAPTER 6. COLDRINKS

The only "fizzy drink" or soft drink you ever need to buy is Coca Cola. Coca Cola was and still is the best stomach medicine in the world. This is largely due to the small percentage of phosphoric acid present in Coca Cola which helps to destroy mal bacteria and viruses which should not be in your stomach. Coca Cola also aids in the digestion of large amounts of food, in particular meat and bread due to again the small amount of phosphoric acid present. Coca Cola is the only soft drink in the world with this characteristic. [Until such time as it has been disproven I will go as far as saying that drinking Coca Cola is a way to treat and prevent Cancer.]

To save money you need to buy concentrates which come in many different flavours from your local supermarket. These should be mixed with cool, filtered water- do not use tap water. These concentrates also come in many delicious fruit flavours so you get your fruit as well. Many people cannot drink the pure fruit juices due to either the high acid content present or are allergic to the preservatives which are used so water based fruit juice is a great alternative. Drinking water based coldrinks and fruit juices not only should save you money but also keep you healthier.

This should save you at least **R200.00** per month = **R2400.00** per annum = **R168000.00** per 70 year lifetime.

CHAPTER 7. BARBEQUE

You should barbeque at least once every week as this is the cheapest and the healthiest way of preparing and cooking meat. The intense heat of the barbeque will destroy any mal bacteria or viruses on the meat and melt a lot of unwanted fat away. Barbequeing or braaing as they say in South Africa is also a healthy and fun outdoor pursuit and can be enjoyed by friends and family. Cooking meat in this way will also save you a lot of money on your electricity bill as any appliance which uses heat also uses a lot of electricity.

You may barbeque anything from meat to desserts- there are many recipe books available which will enable you to cook your entire meal on the barbeque. If you are using a public facility for this please ensure you leave the place neat, clean and tidy and furthermore ensure that no fire or fire hazard is left behind.

Cooking meat in this manner can save you as much as R200.00 per month = R2400.00 per annum = R168000.00 per 70 year lifetime.

CHAPTER 8. HAIRCUTS

You and your family will have to have haircuts at least four times a year. Barbers are charging ridiculous prices for this simple service.

The solution is to buy your own barbers/haircutting kit and get someone in the family to cut your hair. There are many shops which sell these- so shop around for the best prices.

Women can even have their hair styled, permed, etc. all from the comfort of their home at a fraction of the cost of a commercial shop.

Cutting your hair regularly is very important for health and hygiene and to stimulate further hair growth which in men can help with baldness.

D.I.Y. haircuts should save you at least another R200.00 per month = R2400.00 per year = R368000.00 per 70 year lifetime.

CHAPTER 9. TRANSPORT

The petrol price will never decrease, so if you own a "gas guzzler", now is the time to sell it and get a smaller, fuel efficient car.

A motorbike, scooter or even a bicycle are other alternatives to get to work and back.

Using public transport systems are yet another alternative- in some countries these systems are so cheap and efficient there is no need for any other alternative.

Another alternative is to arrange and use a "lift club" to get to work or for the kids to get home from school.

Whatever system you decide to use a money saving should be realized, even as much as R200.00 per month = R2400.00 per year = R168000.00 per 70 year lifetime.

CHAPTER 10. VACATIONS

People tend to spend too much money on holidays, so these need to be carefully planned and budgeted for.

I am not a great fan of time share as these put a noose around your neck from which you can never free yourself.

The best and the cheapest holiday is hiking. Hiking trails are normally quite fully booked, so you need to book early. Hiking is also a healthy, outdoor family pursuit which will keep you fit forever. It is very important to use the right equipment such a hiking boots and to go fully prepared i.e. first aid kit, flares etc.

Another healthy outdoor pursuit is to go camping at a game reserve which can also be relatively inexpensive and can be enjoyed by the whole family. Fishing camps can also be a lot of fun for those who enjoy fishing.

For the sport minded there are always tennis tournaments held throughout the country during the school holidays which are great for the kids to play in and to enjoy. The schedule can be obtained from S.A.T.A. Accommodation at these venues is normally very economical, so there is another great holiday alternative.

Whatever you decide to do for your vacation, make sure you save money, as much as **R200.00 per month = R2400.00 per year = R168000.00 per 70 year lifetime.**

CHAPTER 11. HOMESCHOOL

More and more parents these days are taking the home schooling option as schools are just becoming too expensive.

A lot of the expense can simply be attributed to transport to and from school.

Not only are schools becoming too expensive but a lot of time is actually wasted on "nonsense activities" which do not actually contribute anything whatsoever to the education of your child.

The only drawback is your child will miss out on social interaction with other kids his/her age in a school environment.

The massive advantage is your child will learn to teach himself/herself and will be much better prepared for university.

Your child will also learn things he/she would not have learnt at school.

The best option is to get a group together in your neighbourhood who can do home schooling together.

Home schooling should save a further R200.00 per month = R2400.00 annum = R168000.00 per 70 year lifetime.

CHAPTER 12. WORK FROM HOME

Nowadays more and more people are able to work from home as more and more jobs are being "outsourced." This means that most companies have a workforce at the factory or worksite and a workforce at home. This has been made possible by the **PC** and modern technology.

If you are one of those fortunate people who work from home there are many benefits and cost savings. There are the obvious health benefits of working in a "healthy" environment without the stress of a boss- employee relationship. Then there is the cost savings regarding petrol, lunches, vehicle maintenance and others.

All of these should account for a savings of R200.00 per month = R2400.00 per annum = R168000.00 per 70 year lifetime.

CHAPTER 13. D.I.Y.

A lot of small jobs around the home can easily be done by yourself, whether they be building, electrical, plumbing or just general maintenance. There is absolutely no need to get and pay a professional to do certain small jobs. Most hardware stores are well set up and stock everything you may need to do the job.

D.I.Y. books may also be purchased which detail exactly what you need to do the job plus the tools and materials required. These books also make excellent gifts for the handyman.

Doing your own home maintenance should easily save you R200.00 per month = R2400.00 per year = R168000.00 per 70 year lifetime.

CHAPTER 14. INTERNET BANKING

Internet banking fees are far cheaper than any other means of doing your banking. Whether you use your PC or cellphone it can be done quickly and easily from any location. You can make and receive payments as well as do some online shopping where your products (in some cases) are delivered to your door.

This will save you petrol expense plus the hassle of standing in queues at the bank.

Doing your banking online can easily save you **R200.00** per month = **R2400.00** per annum = **R168000.00** per 70 year lifetime.

CHAPTER 15. MOTOR VEHICLE REPAIRS.

If you know something about mechanical/electrical repairs or have a friend who knows then you can save a lot of money by purchasing a replacement part and doing the work yourselves. There are also people who do this work from their garages and only charge a small fee.

If your car has rust damage and is ten years or older then you must do the repair work yourself as it will not pay you to spend money on such a vehicle. The simple fact of the matter is that it will rust again within four years.

Nowadays anything and everything to do with your car costs money so the more you and your friends can do the more you can save.

By doing as much as you can "yourself" you can easily save up to R200.00 per month = R2400.00 per annum = R168000.00 per 70 year lifetime.

CHAPTER 16. CUTTING LUXURIES

If you're a smoker, you need to kick the habit- if you consume alcohol regularly you need to cut down to just one drink on the weekend. People who plead poverty still drink and smoke- multi billion rand industries have ben created out of this simple fact of life.

Belonging to a Sports Club and paying excessive fees for playing is out- the only exercise you ever need your entire life is walking. The same goes for gyms or for other "exercise equipment". The simple fact of the matter is you don't need it.

Restrict your chocolate consumption to just one bar on the weekend- it must be a treat. Some people will go as far as saying if you can't afford a chocolate then you might just as well slit your throat.

Dining out as a family outing must be restricted to perhaps only once per month- the same can be said for purchasing "take aways."

Swallowing thousands of vitamins or health supplements is just stupid- you need to cut that out.

The only time you need to purchase new clothes is if your old clothes are either too small or are worn out. If you're an adult and your clothes are too small it means you're too fat so you need to cut down on your eating.

Implementing these simple ideas could easily save you **R200.00 per month = R2400 per annum = R168000 per 70 year lifetime.**

CHAPTER 17. HOME GENERATORS

Home generators can be a worthwhile investment considering the cost of electricity and the worldwide energy crisis.

Ryobi manufacture a relatively inexpensive generator which is petrol or diesel driven and is not big and heavy like their competitors in the market.

It might even become cheaper to power your entire home on a generator rather than use electricity. If you use a generator you should run it for one entire day once a week to "power up your grid" with "free electricity" so that you can run without using your national power supply for a while.

Though still in an experimental stage "free energy devices" are taking the world by storm. These devices can be built in your garage using simple materials from your local hardware store.

These devices use such concepts as perpetual motion, gravity and magnetism to power their motors.

This is the future and you are a part of it.

Using a generator can easily save you R200.00 per month = R2400.00 per annum = R168000.00 per 70 year lifetime.

CHAPTER 18. TOTAL SAVINGS

By incorporating and implementing these simple ideas into your daily lives a staggering R3400.00 per month = R40800.00 per annum = R2,85600 million may be saved.

Saving money is definitely a worthwhile strategy to adopt.

www.ingramcontent.com/pod-product-compliance
Lightning Source LLC
Chambersburg PA
CBHW021852170526
45157CB00006B/2413